THE WHOLE WIDE WORLD

How can we learn about and care for the world?

page 4

Literature

page 20

READING ACROSS TEXTS

Related Readings and Projects

When All the World's Asleep

By Anita E. Posey

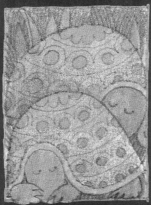

Where do insects go at night,
When all the world's asleep?
Where do bugs and butterflies
And caterpillars creep?
Turtles sleep inside their shells;
The robin has her nest.
Rabbits and the sly old fox
Have holes where they can rest.
Bears can crawl inside a cave;
The lion has his den.
Cows can sleep inside the barn,
And pigs can use their pen.
But where do bugs and butterflies
And caterpillars creep,
When everything is dark outside
And all the world's asleep?

Homes in Danger

"When All the World's Asleep" describes animals' homes, or habitats. Some habitats are endangered. They are in danger of being destroyed. Three of these habitats are Pacific Northwest forests, coral reefs, and rain forests. Find out more about endangered habitats and how you can help save them.

Gather Information

1. Do research to learn about one of the endangered habitats above, or choose one of your own. Ask a science teacher or librarian for help.

2. Make a list of questions about the habitat. Include questions such as:

- Where is the habitat located?
- How is it being endangered?
- What is happening to the animals that live there?
- What can people do to help?

3. Take notes as you look for and find answers.

Organize and Draw Conclusions

4. Look over your notes. Organize your ideas into categories, such as location, problems, and ideas to help. Then ask yourself: What is the best way to share this information? What facts would get people interested in helping out?

Write and Present

5. How will you present your information? You could create bumper stickers and posters, write a public service announcement, or deliver a radio talk. Think of how to reach people with your message! Present your work to the class.

All I See

Story by Cynthia Rylant — Pictures by Peter Catalanotto

There once was a man named Gregory who spent his days beside a lake painting pictures. He wore an old gray raincoat when he painted, and two brushes were tucked behind his ears. Sometimes as he worked he also whistled Beethoven's Fifth Symphony very loudly, waving his brush in the air through the exciting parts. Gregory's white cat lay beside him, sleeping through it all, the painting and the symphony.

When Gregory tired of working and whistling, he picked up his cat, climbed into a canoe, and paddled off down the lake.

He lay flat on his back in the bottom of the drifting boat, staring straight up at the sky.

A boy named Charlie who summered at the lake used to watch Gregory paint and whistle and drift in his canoe with his cat. Charlie had decided he was fond of Gregory, though they had never met.

One day when Gregory was out in his canoe, Charlie sneaked a look at the picture Gregory was painting.

Charlie was surprised by what he saw, by what
Gregory had painted as he looked at Charlie's lake.
   But the picture made Charlie like Gregory even more.
   So each day when Gregory drifted away, Charlie
sneaked a look. And each day Charlie saw the same thing;
a blue whale. Sometimes the whale was diving in deep

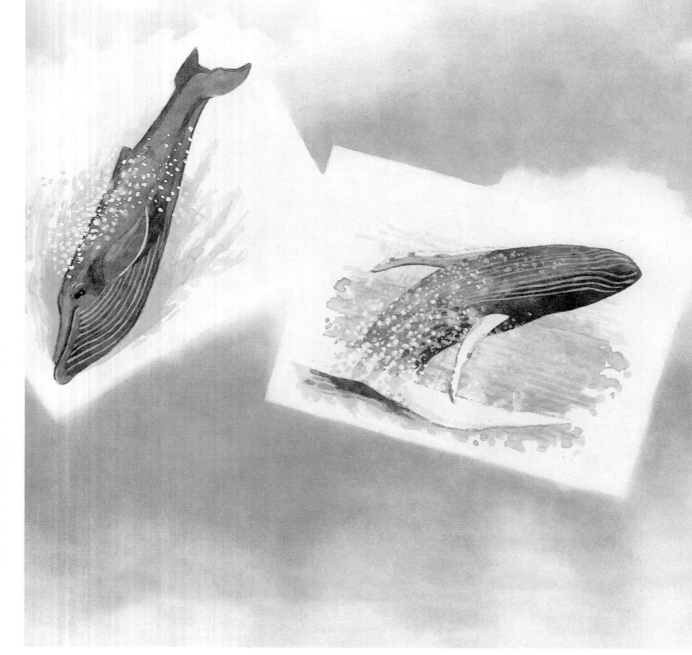

water, sometimes it was leaping up out of the water, sometimes it was upside down. But it was always a whale.

And Charlie became fond of whales too.

But one morning when Gregory was away, Charlie found nothing on the canvas. No painting. No whale. No picture for Charlie.

So while Gregory drifted far off down the lake, staring at the sea-blue sky and humming Beethoven's Fifth, Charlie picked up a brush.

While Gregory stroked his sleeping white cat, Charlie squeezed out some paint.

And while Gregory rested and hummed, Charlie painted.

He left his picture there for Gregory. Charlie was too shy, and afraid, to stay.

When he paddled back to shore, Gregory was astonished to find a painting on his easel. He was even more astonished to see himself in the painting, standing at the easel, white cat sleeping, and musical notes bouncing all over the sky.

Gregory sat and stared at that painting for a long time.

The next day when Gregory went far off down the lake, Charlie again sneaked a look and again found no blue whale. But this time, painted on Gregory's canvas were these words: I LIKED THE PICTURE.

Charlie picked up the brush. He was smiling and his heart pounded as he painted: THANK YOU.

Again, he was too shy, and afraid, to stay.

The following day there was a new message:

PLEASE
STAY !

So Charlie stayed. And when Gregory paddled back to shore, he wiped his hands on his old gray raincoat, shook Charlie's hand, and introduced Stella, his cat.

For many days after that, Gregory and Charlie were at the lake together. Gregory taught Charlie about shadows and light, about line, about drawing things near and things far away.

He also taught Charlie how to scratch Stella under the chin without getting clawed.

And, of course, Gregory allowed Charlie to paint. Charlie painted whatever he saw. He painted everything he saw, there on the lake.

Gregory did not paint at all during this time.

Then one day Gregory waited for Charlie with a gift. He had brought for Charlie an easel of his own, and new brushes, and new paints, and clean canvases.

They stood side by side then, that day, brushes tucked behind their ears, painting. Gregory painted a blue whale floating in seaweed full of tiny pink fish. Charlie painted whatever he saw.

At the end of the day, Charlie finally asked Gregory why he painted only whales.

Gregory's face opened up into an enormous smile. He looked out across the water and he said, "It is all I see." He smiled for a long time.

Charlie, too, looked out across the water, and he knew Gregory's whales were there somewhere. He also knew that something was waiting for him, waiting to be seen and to be painted.

Cynthia Rylant

Cynthia Rylant, the author of *All I See*, was raised in the mountains of West Virginia. She used this setting for her first book, *When I Was Young in the Mountains*. Since then, Ms. Rylant has written more than forty books for children and young adults. Her own illustrations appear in some of her books. She also has published magazine articles and poems.

Look at Author's Craft

When you read Cynthia Rylant's writing, look for these characteristics:

Strong images Ms. Rylant uses words in a way that helps readers form vivid pictures in their minds as they read.

Familiar characters Most of her characters are everyday people, like her neighbors and friends from her childhood in West Virginia. In *The Blue Hill Meadows*, Rylant tells about a typical family and how their lives change during the four seasons of the year.

Focus on friendship Many of her stories focus on friendship. Gregory and Charlie in *All I See*, for example, develop a friendship because they both love art.

Read More and Share

Read more books by Cynthia Rylant. As you read, think about the strong images, familiar characters, and the friendships between characters.

The Bookshop Dog When a bookshop owner has to go to the hospital, everyone in town wants to take care of her adorable dog.

Gooseberry Park Read about the adventures of Stumpy Squirrel and her babies, Kona the dog, Murray the bat, and Gwendolyn the hermit crab.

The Blue Hill Meadows The warm, humorous story of Willie Meadows and his family

Now think about what you read. Find examples of strong images and friendships between characters. Make a list and share it with the class.

Pick a Painting

Gregory and Charlie like paintings of whales. Think of a painting that you like. How could you explain why you like it? Gather your ideas as you prepare a short speech about why you like your painting.

What You Do

1. Look for a painting that you like. If you find one in a library book, check the book out so you can show the painting as you speak.

2. Why do you like the painting? List at least three specific things that you like about this painting. Think about things like colors, shapes, light and shadow, faces, expressions. How does the painting make you feel? Why? Make notes on your ideas.

3. Find out more about the painting, the artist, and other paintings this person has done. You might ask someone you know, look in art books, or go to an art museum.

4. Present your painting to the class. Use your notes to tell about the painting and the artist. Include your own opinions about the painting as well.

Use What You Learn

5. Get together with classmates and create a class art gallery with your paintings and notes.

Red Leaf, Yellow Leaf

by Lois Ehlert

first spring leaf

I've been saving this little leaf from my sugar maple tree so I could show it to you. I love my tree.

It was born long before I was. The wind blew seeds from the big maple trees in the woods. They twirled and whirled as they fell to the ground.

Seeds the squirrels didn't find lay sleeping among the leaves until they were covered with snow.

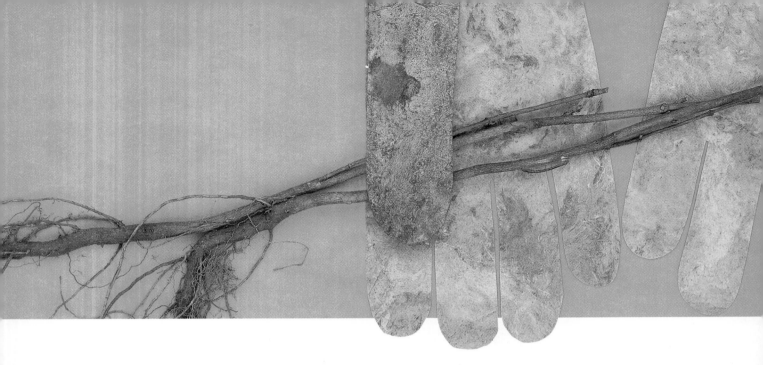

When spring sun warmed the seeds, they sprouted
and sent roots down into the soil. Tiny leaves unfolded on
their stems.

I think my tree would've been happy to stay there forever.
But one day nursery workers came to the woods to collect
tree sprouts.

They transplanted the sprouts and tended them year
after year.

Just as the trees were settling in, they were measured, marked, and uprooted again!

Each ball of roots was wrapped and tied with twine.

My tree was loaded onto a truck filled with other trees and delivered to the garden center.

We went there in the fall and picked out my tree.

Dad had a hole, already dug, waiting for it.

When we got home, we lowered my tree into the hole. I held the trunk while Dad covered the roots with soil.

Now every night before I go to bed, I peek out the window
and wave to my tree. When it snows, I hang up treats for
the birds.

Each spring, I look for signs that my tree is growing. By
late summer, the crown of leaves is bushy and green. I love
it when the tree flowers turn into winged seeds. But if you
want to visit my tree, come in the fall. That's my favorite
time. Can you guess why?

Leaves

Leaves get their green color from a pigment called chlorophyll that helps them absorb sunlight. In a process called photosynthesis, leaves use water, energy from sunlight, and carbon dioxide from the air to make a type of sugar the tree needs for food. When leaves produce this sugar, they also give off oxygen, which purifies the air we breathe.

Maple leaves have other pigments too. As days get shorter and temperatures cool down, the tree begins to rest. It stops making chlorophyll, and other pigments color the leaves red, orange, and yellow. This is a sign that the tree is getting ready for winter and will soon drop its leaves.

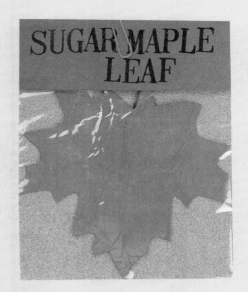

SUGAR MAPLE LEAF

Buds

Buds on maple tree branches grow in pairs, one on each side of the stem. Some buds, usually the larger ones, grow into flowers, and others become leaves.

Roots and Sap

Roots are like underground branches that absorb minerals and water from the soil. The first root that the tree develops is called the taproot. As new roots grow, the taproot and older roots that grow out from it act as anchors so the tree doesn't tip over as it gets taller. The roots have root hairs along their sides, which feed the tree by absorbing nutrients such as water and minerals. The nutrients flow from the roots out to the branches through pipelike passages in the trunk. In early spring, while maple trees are still leafless and temperatures moderate, the sweet fluid called sap begins to run, feeding the tree buds. During this time a big maple tree, at least twelve inches in diameter, can be tapped without stressing the tree by drilling a hole in the bark and inserting a spout. Sap from the tree drips out through the hole. It is collected in a container and later boiled down to make maple syrup and sugar.

Bark

Bark is the outer skin of a tree. It protects the tree's interior from injury by animals and insects.

Tree Flowers

Maple trees bloom in the spring at about the same time that the leaves begin to appear. The flowers later become seeds.

Seeds

Maple tree seeds grow in winged seed cases called samaras, which develop out of the spring flowers. The seeds mature three or four months after the tree flowers fade. When the samaras drop off the trees, they spin on their wings and twirl as they fall to the ground. If they land in just the right spot, they will begin to grow. Each seed contains everything it needs to start a new tree. Birds, squirrels, and other small animals love to eat the seeds.

Planting a Tree

Selecting the Right Tree

Before going to the garden center, decide what kind of tree you want. You might see one you like as you take a walk or visit a park. You could also check seed catalogs or reference books at the library. Try to learn as much as you can about your tree before you bring it home. Consider where you will plant it and how large it will grow. Also be sure the tree you want will grow well in your climate and soil. If you pick a sugar maple like the one in this book, remember you might be the one who has to rake the red and yellow leaves in the fall.

Planting Times

The best time for planting trees is when they are dormant, or resting. This would be spring, before leaves develop, or fall, after the leaves drop off. These times are the least stressful for the tree, but trees can also be planted in summer if given plenty of water. Winter isn't usually suggested in cold areas where the ground freezes.

Preparing the Tree Site

You may want to dig a hole before you go to the garden center so it's ready for your tree when you bring it home. You will need to know approximately how big the root ball will be. Usually the hole should be twice as wide and one and a half times as deep as the root ball. While transplanting the tree, it is important to keep the roots moist at all times.

SUGAR MAPLE

Planting the Tree

After the hole is dug, put a mixture of peat moss and topsoil on the bottom. Add just enough so that when you put the root ball inside, its top will be level with the surrounding ground. A tree is heavier than it looks; it usually takes two adults to lift one. Pick up the tree by its root ball and gently lower it into the hole. Then cut the twine, loosen the burlap, and roll it back. Leave the burlap around the bottom of the root ball. It will decompose. Fill in the space around the root ball with soil, and make a ridge of soil around the edge of the hole. This ridge will help retain water near the tree's roots. Then water the tree thoroughly. You will need to continue to water your new tree regularly—sometimes twice a week in hot weather.

Wrapping

Wrapping the trunk of a new tree with burlap strips or tree tape protects its delicate bark from sun scald. It also prevents deer, rabbits, squirrels, and other animals from chewing the bark. You should leave the wrapping on for about two years.

Staking

If your tree trunk is larger than one inch in diameter, it needs to be supported with stakes so it won't tip over. Pound wooden stakes into the ground near the trunk and then tie them to the trunk with soft rope or burlap strips.

Red leaf,
Yellow leaf,
Beautiful tree
Love,
from
me

What's That Tree?

In *Red Leaf, Yellow Leaf,* the child plants a sugar maple tree. Look at the shape of the sugar maple's leaf. A maple leaf is different from other leaves. It has its own special shape.

Imagine that you work at a forest preserve. Make a field-guide pamphlet that hikers can take with them to identify the trees they see on their nature walk.

What You Need

books about leaves

drawing paper

tracing paper

crayons or colored pencils

What You Do

1. Use reference books about leaves to find the shapes of different leaves.

2. Choose several different leaves. Draw them for your pamphlet. (You might want to use tracing paper.) Color the leaves as they appear in the reference book.

3. Below each leaf drawing, write the name of the tree and some interesting facts about it. Put your pages together into a pamphlet.

Use What You Learn

4. Use your pamphlet to identify the trees in your yard, near the school, or in a nearby park or forest preserve. Which trees can you find? Are there trees in your pamphlet that don't grow near where you live? Where would you need to travel to find these trees?

What Good Is a Tree?

For people in different parts of the world, trees have different uses. For example:

• In Brazil, workers make cuts in the bark of rubber trees. The liquid that flows from the cuts is used to make rubber.

• In the past, Native Americans in North America used the light, strong bark of birch trees to make canoes. Today, birch is used to make wood products, such as furniture.

• The sap from maple trees is used to make syrup. In eastern Canada, sugar maple is one of the most important crops. How are trees important in your part of the world?

What You Do

1. Find out what trees are used for in your part of the world. Look around your community. Ask teachers, relatives, and friends for ideas.

2. Make a list of all the things you can think of that are made from trees—their sap, their leaves, their bark, their wood, their flowers, their fruit.

3. Make a list of other things that people use trees for, such as climbing and shade.

4. Share your lists with the class.

Use What You Learn

5. Look over your lists and imagine what your world would be like without trees. What would be missing? How could you replace what was missing? Share your thoughts with the class.

Do Plants Really Eat?

Plants take carbon dioxide from the air to make food. When they do this, they create oxygen. This process is called photosynthesis. It is explained under "Leaves" on page 25 of *Red Leaf, Yellow Leaf*. How would you explain photosynthesis to a small child? Think about creating a puppet show to tell the story of photosynthesis.

What You Do

1. Make your puppets. They might include a leaf, a tree, the sun, a bird, a forest ranger. You could make your puppets out of several different kinds of materials. You could use old socks, milk cartons, craft sticks, construction paper—whatever works for you. You might want to make some sort of puppet stage as well.

2. Write a script for your puppet show. A script tells what each character will say in your show, from start to finish. Each puppet character should help explain photosynthesis. Remember, your audience is small children, so keep your explanations simple.

3. Perform your show for a younger brother, sister, or friend. Or you might arrange to perform it for a whole class of younger children.

Use What You Learn

4. When you finish, ask your audience about the show. What did they learn about photosynthesis? Have them explain the process in their own words. How well did your show work? How could you make it better next time?

Reader Response

1. Think About the Theme

How can we learn about and care for the world? List five different things that you learned from the selections in this book about caring for the world. Then ask yourself how you think the world will be in ten years. What will happen to the trees? the whales? Write your answers.

2. Ask a Question

Imagine that you could interview Gregory. What would you ask him about whales and his art? Use the questions and answers to write a short skit. Perform it with a partner.

3. Use New Vocabulary

List new or interesting words that you learned from the selections in this book. Classify them into categories, such as Words About Art, Words About Plants, and so on. Then use words from one category to make a fill-in-the-blanks quiz.

4. Make Connections

Imagine that Charlie, in *All I See*, had read *Red Leaf, Yellow Leaf*. How do you think he would feel about the book? Write your answer as if you were Charlie.

5. Analyze

Imagine that you were at the lake, watching Gregory paint. How would you try to become Gregory's friend? What would you like about being his friend? Would you want to know Charlie? Why or why not? Record your thoughts in a journal entry.